*Dedicated to Janet Lederman
and the past and present teachers who have kept
the dream of Gazebo alive.*

TRUSTING THE INNER TEACHER

Inside Stories of Gazebo Park School

by January Handl

Esalen

Trusting the Inner Teacher
Copyright © 2014 by Janary Handl

All rights reserved. No part of this book may be reproduced, stored in a retrieval system, or transmitted, in any form or by any means, electronic, mechanical, photocopying, recording, or otherwise, without the prior permission of the author.

Contributing photographers: Doug Ellis, David Gilmore

Book design: David Gilmore

ISBN 978-1-935914-48-8

Printed in the United States of America

Additional copies available from:
www.riversanctuarypublishing.com

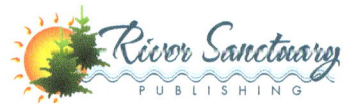

RIVER SANCTUARY PUBLISHING
P.O. Box 1561
Felton, CA 95018
www.riversanctuarypublishing.com

Dedicated to the awakening of the New Earth

INTRODUCTION

These stories and musings were written in my first year as Teacher/Director at Gazebo Park School. It was a wild and transformative year, and the blessings and discomforts of "un-learning" led to insights and delights that were too rich to be kept to myself. Most were published first on the Gazebo Park School Facebook page. The comments led to connections that we, in the early childhood field, count on to hold us through the challenges of an often-undervalued profession. The hope is that by illuminating the magic that is Gazebo, others may be inspired in their work. May the children be seen and heard as the magnificent beings they are!

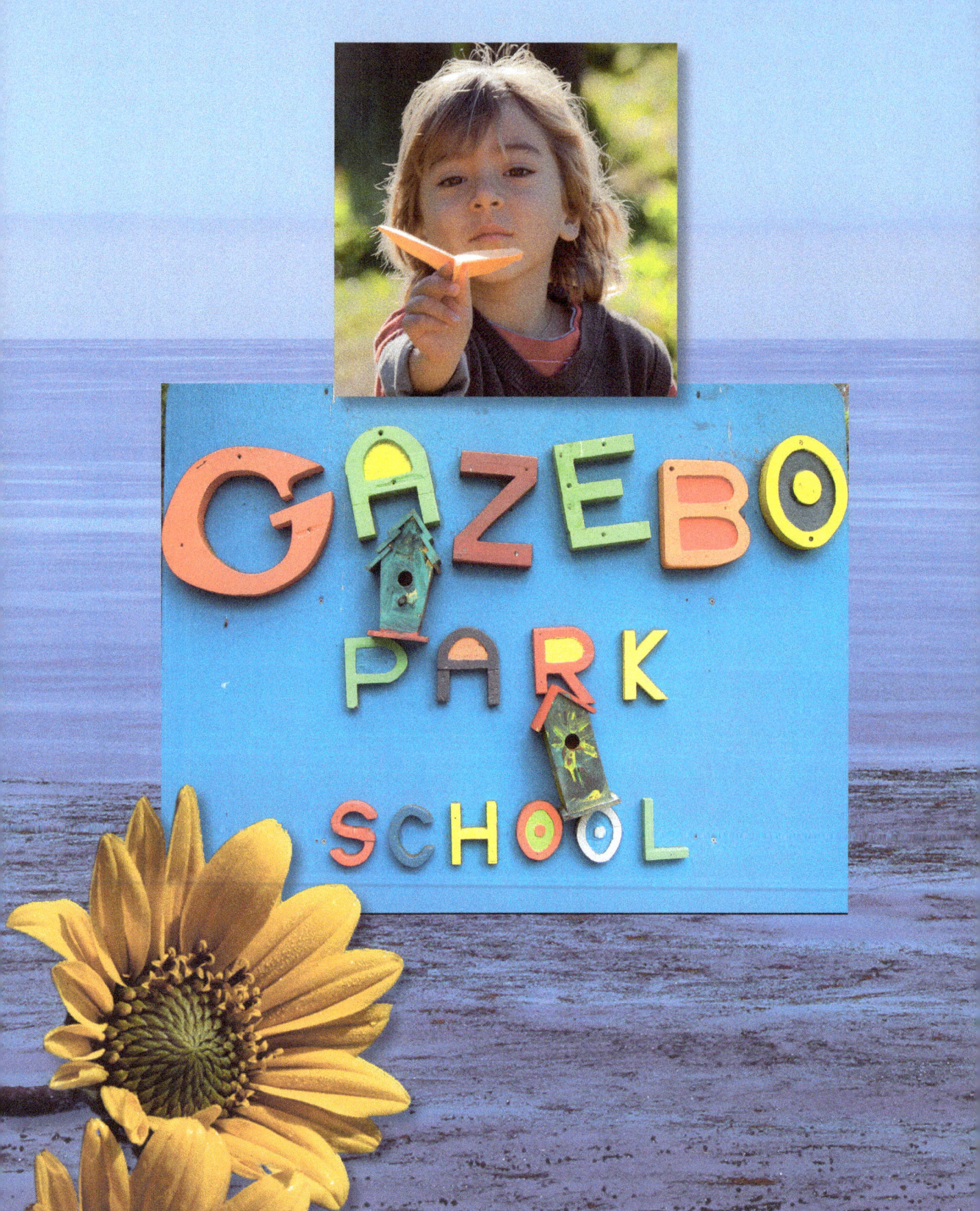

GAZEBO TENETS

- A child who is able to pay attention, attend to what he or she is doing with awareness, will be a successful learner. We *teach* paying attention by *paying* attention.

- As the child attends to his or her learning, we are careful not to intrude.

- The environment is there to maximize the body experiences….it has slopes grades, terraces, and many textures, to give a varied body experience from moment-to-moment. It is an environment that rewards the child for every movement.

- The Gazebo is designed with the educational goal of maximizing the FULL use of the child's growing body and unfolding intelligence.

- Some children learn by exploring everything, some by staying in one area; some learn by touching all objects, others by building around them familiar items; some are more interested in pouring water and others in slopping it. All of these proclivities balance and change in time.

- Gazebo is a place where children explore who they are, what they can do, and how they feel – *apart* from parents….and in doing so discover who they are, what they can do, and how they feel…*with* parents.

- The philosophy involves the integration of generations, the inviting of children back into society, and the re-introduction of living in to the content of learning.

- The Gazebo is always in the process of organization and development.

- The tools for gardening and developing the land are critical learning materials. The landscaping and surprise developments become the overall learning project for the children, the staff, and the neighbors.

- When experience and learning are partners, resourcefulness follows.

— Janet Lederman 1979

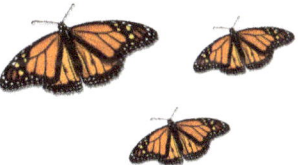

FIRST DAYS AT GAZEBO

Gazebo is growing me. This past week a child who seeks heavy physical tasks, and also has a deep-thinking, quick-moving mind, started his own project. He had gotten into a few destructive, slightly mischievous activities the previous week, and we, as a staff, had spoken about looking for ways to support who he is in the world, while preserving materials for everyone.

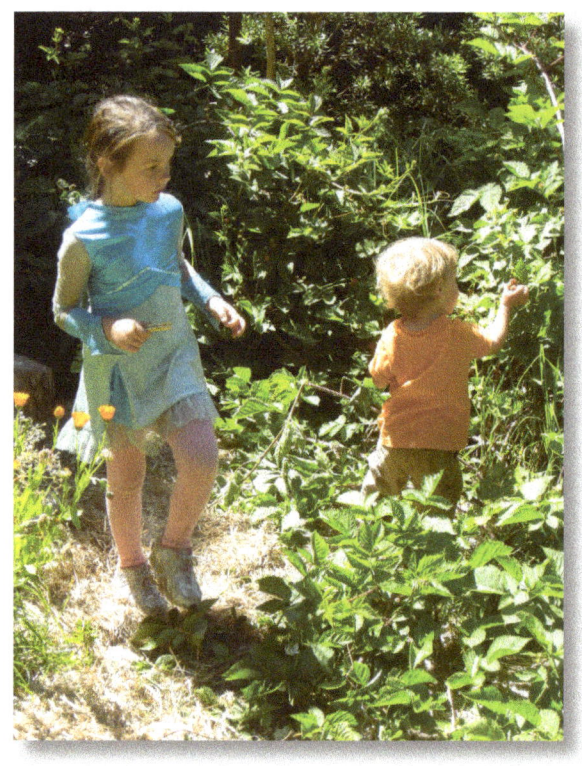

He began by prying off the outer bark of an old stump. A teacher moved closer, and thinking out loud about the stump beginning to rot, got the child gloves and a tool to do deeper work. As he pried and hammered and splintered the decaying stump, layers of decomposers came to the surface: ants, giant termites, termite babies, and even a salamander were uncovered and held and observed. Soon several children joined in the work, and I moved over to talk about the difference between tools and toys, and safety space needed in such endeavors. The children seemed to relish this deconstruction, and every discovery on the way. I enjoyed peering into the cycles of life with them.

Later, a more veteran Gazebo teacher gently talked to me about supporting health and safety, while preserving children's direct experiences as the deepest teachers — perhaps asking questions more than stating safety zones (allowing the sensory and physical discoveries their own unfurling and questions before offering my own).

I am in awe of what Gazebo can grow in even the oldest of students and teachers.

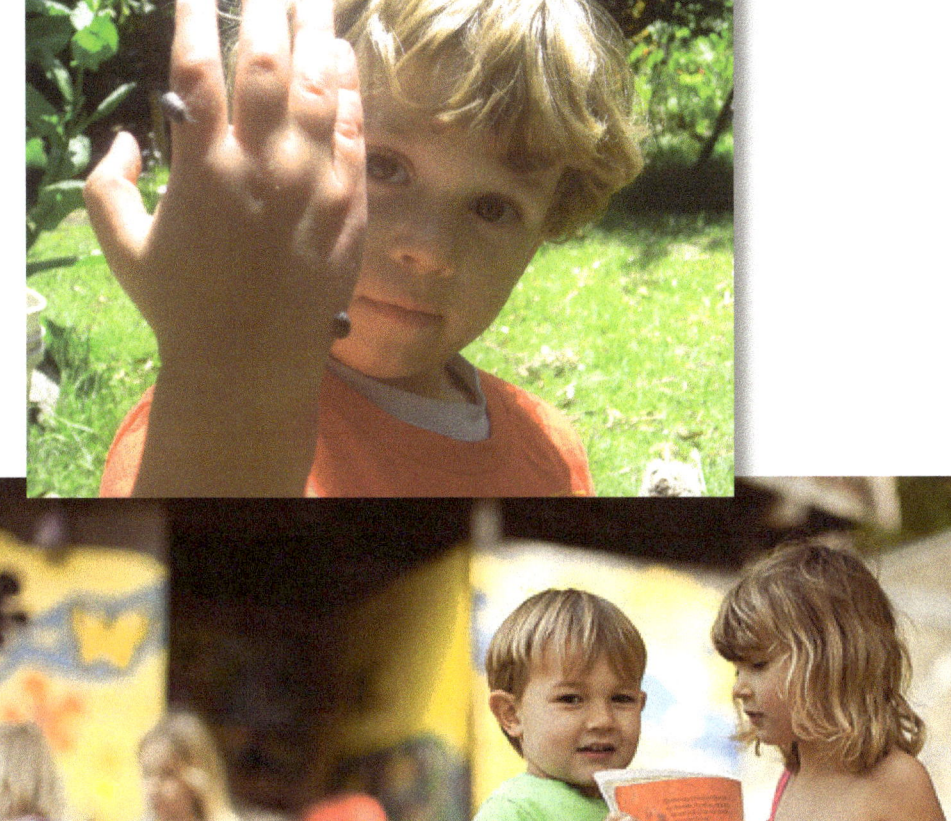

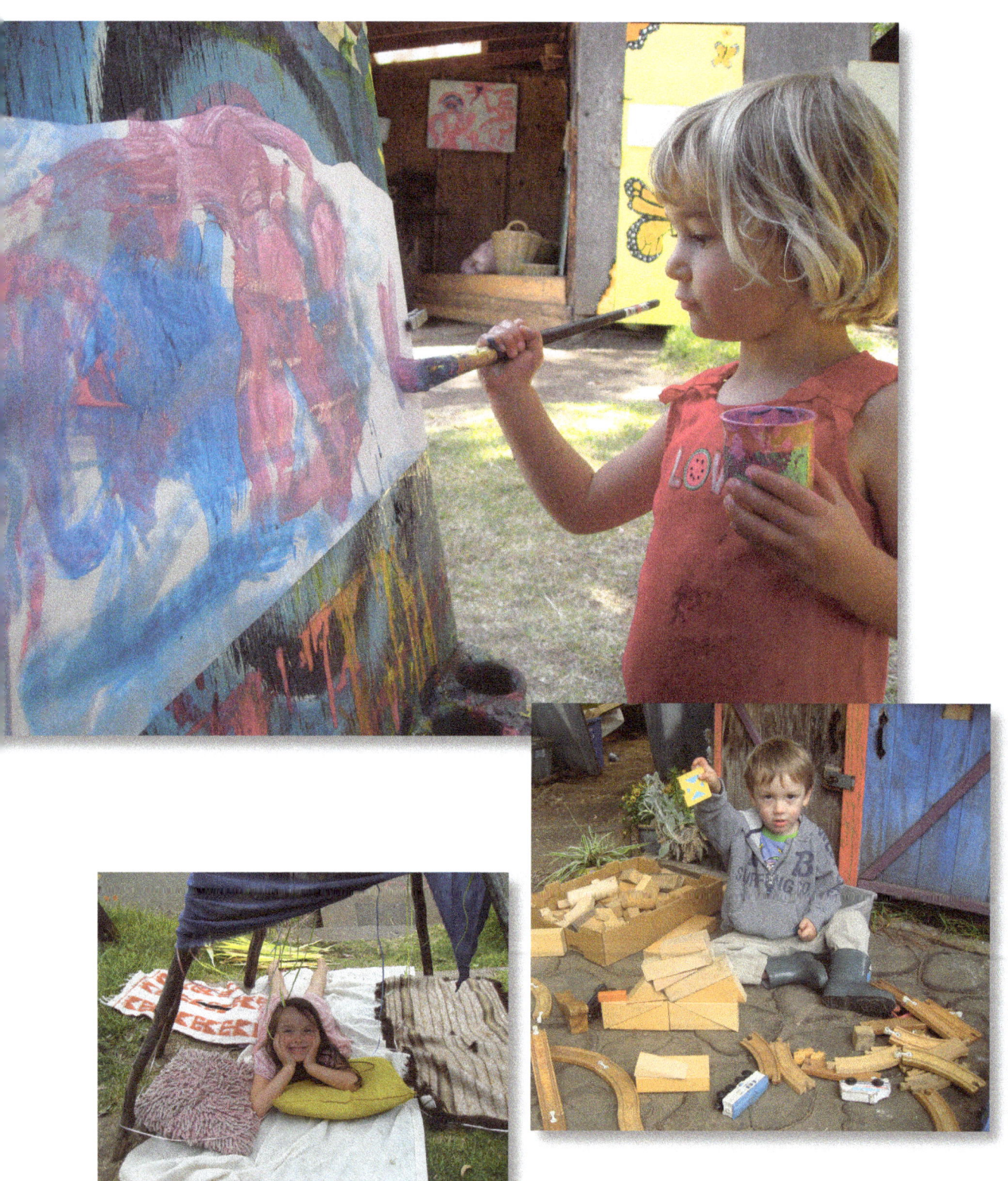

THE VIEW OF THE CHILD

One of the things that made me feel most at home at Gazebo was that the philosophy's view of the child so closely matched my own. On a deep intuitive level I've always seen young people, from birth until adulthood, as whole beings. Different levels of experience, different opportunities and environment, different biochemistry, and differing meanings given to shared experiences and relationship. Somehow each person has some part of their selfhood that is basically intact from the moment they are born. The inner teacher and hard-wired drive to learn/make meaning are parts of the package with which we come into this world. Some of the deepest sadness I have felt regarding education is when I witness the slow death or distortion of a child's own way of knowing. It often manifests as a sense of dividedness — the face that is shown to the outside world in order to conform, please, and fit into entrenched systems and culture, often does not reflect the inner experience of the individual. Without our own experience honored and given space and time, we begin to question our own direct understanding and hand over our birthright unique lens and expression. We learn to shut down the body's messages to us, to move our perceptions all up into our heads, quickly sifting out anything that doesn't match what others (especially others who have more power than us) are telling us we are "allowed" to experience. Learning styles are often ignored, and children aren't spoken to, they are spoken about.

In addition, Gazebo not only holds space for a child's experience and the teacher's experience, but also sees the child as capable, or even, as a matter of fact, built for the struggle to develop toward full potential. In other words, children are trusted. Trusted to make choices and learn from those choices. Trusted to be able to build on foundations of learning and constructed world views as they are allowed to engage with each other, the teachers and the natural world around them. They are trusted to have the curiosity to form their own questions and direction of discovery. And, they are trusted with all of their feelings. Not without support, compassion and reflection from the adults who are caring for them — but without trying to distract or dismiss every feeling that may be uncomfortable. Children are trusted as self-guided play masters, who naturally

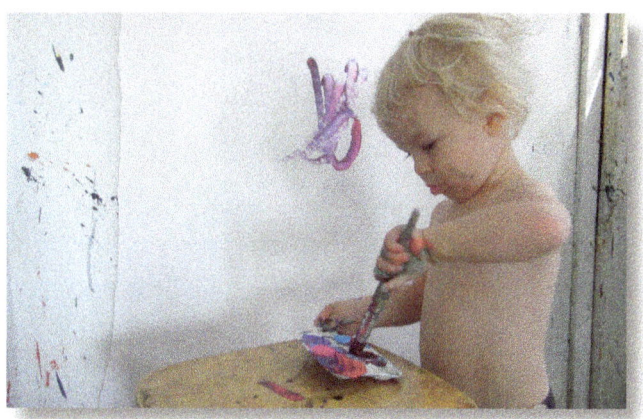

push themselves to the next level in all areas of development. Their accomplishments and skills mastered are reflected back to them for the innate "ah hah!" sense of intrinsic reward that provides them with the motivation to take further risks along their own progression toward growth.

Since it is inevitable that we adults are looked at by children as the mirrors of who they are, we have the deep responsibility to reflect our view of each child as capable, trust-worthy, equipped for struggle and growth, and full-feeling beings who deserve love and support by the growing/learning beings who are their "teachers." A humbling endeavor that asks the very best of us as well.

THE ROLE OF THE TEACHER

Our current intern at Gazebo asked me a question the answer to which is beyond quite what can be explained in words, in language. "At Gazebo, what is the role of the teacher?" Of course there are standard answers that apply: mentor, guide, leader, safety monitor, nurse, giver of knowledge, servant.

As I sat with the question one morning, the thought of dance partners kept coming to me, and the twist is that even though the teacher is the more experienced, learned, and developed dancer, the child gets to – must – take the lead in the partner-ship. And there are no pre-set steps to each moment's dance.

One of the most unique aspects of Gazebo is the overlay of Gestalt theory and practice. It is acknowledged that whatever the setting, the curriculum, the philosophy, the student and teacher are a part of the equation. Their life experiences, biochemistry and ways of knowing are the "x" factor in the algebraic equation that becomes the constant flow of energy in the park.

The learning, un-learning, the shared experiences, the facts, the truth, and the dialogue with nature, are all perceived and given meaning in very different ways by each person involved.

Most teachers in any setting know at some core level, that indeed, we are "teaching" human beings, not curriculum, and without the nod toward the student's interests, motivations and learning styles, very little gets learned. Or worse, what gets learned is a coercive sort of giving up of personal power and the individual's birthright to pursue truth and happiness. The teacher, too, especially needs to be noticing how their own woundings and strengths are coming into play, not to dismiss them, but to use a consciousness of them to "teach" with some clarity.

Just like being a parent, the role of the teacher at Gazebo is the art of stepping back. We strive to be the bridge for learning and then dissolve that particular structure as the child shows us that we are no longer needed. There is another critical aspect of being a teacher that aligns with the role of the parent. At Gazebo we have the

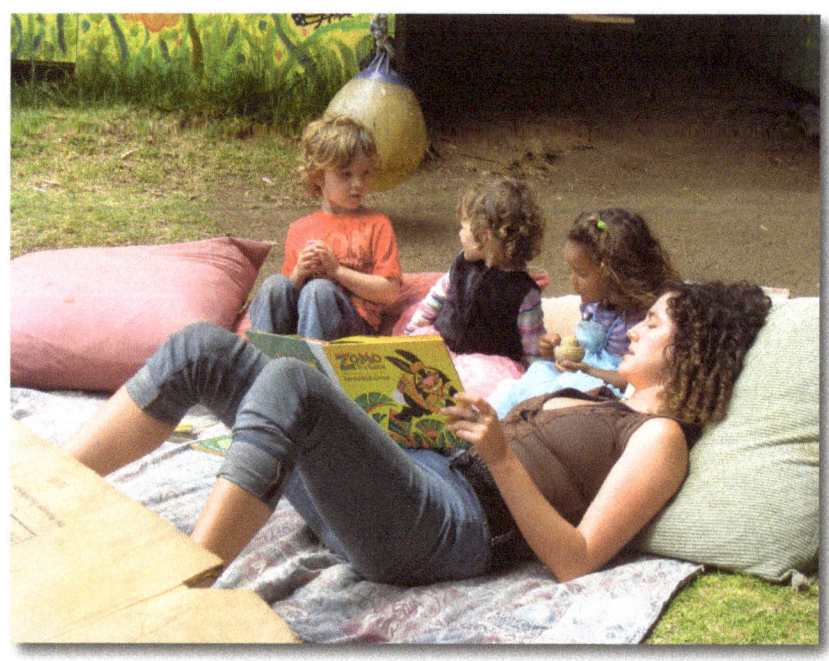

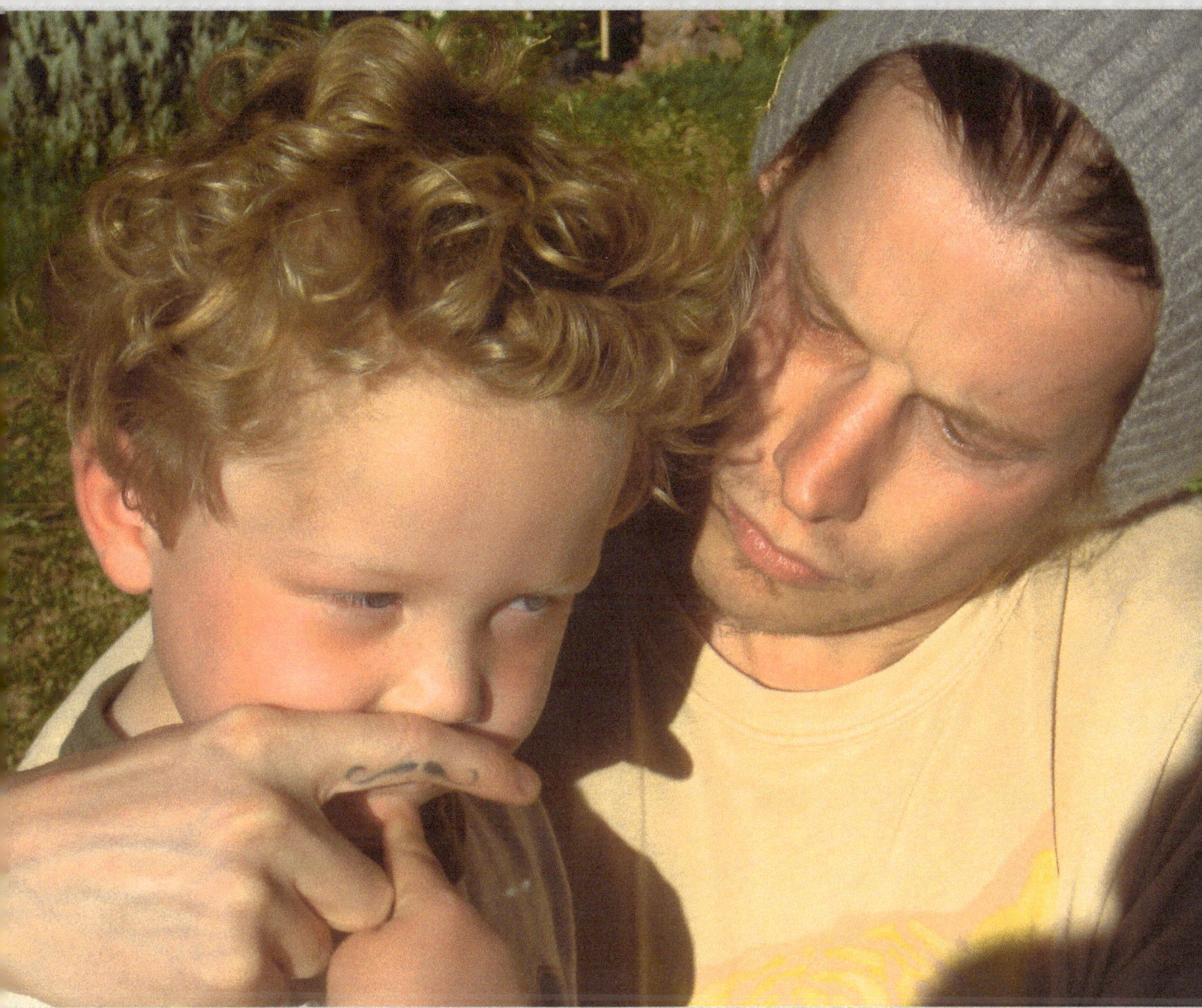

good fortune to be in a community that offers a structure of Gestalt process and inner work that provides us with a means to accomplish one of the greatest challenges and bounties of being a teacher: that of knowing ourselves deeply.

I often tell parents and teachers for whom I am facilitating trainings, that they will inevitably teach/parent who we are. We cannot help it, it will occur. And so our grave responsibility and deepest work is to know ourselves. To know when who we are is serving us, and when it is getting in the way of our goals and relationships. And then help children with this same life-long tool of self-reflection. The greatest teachers are perennial learners...of themselves, of their own students, of the offerings of continued study, pedagogy, and growth.

It is very hard work! It is rich with opportunity for learning in each dance partner. No formula or theory can quite define what happens in the dance as the music changes or the dancers develop and grow. I am grateful to be a part of the miraculous pedagogy, as the line between dancers blurs and becomes simply: the beautiful dance of inter-being!

KIDS, KIDS, KIDS

The title above is on every agenda of every staff meeting we hold at Gazebo. There is always so much business that any staff needs to cover to run a quality child care program, it is easy to let this, our very reason for being, slip.

Whether it is one of our lovely 3 year old's recent grabs for power at the possible expense of our youngest, or the resistance to visit Pottyville for a toileting toddler, or a slow-to-warm up child's triumph over fears, we all find these conversations to be the best part of any meeting.

Currently we have been working toward figuring out what a certain 2-1/2 year old is working on or through. We bring up our own triggers and pet peeves, our theories and ideas, our bewilderment or exasperation. We bring up humorous moments, and joyful discoveries. We come up with a tentative approach for the trial and error ways true teachers must have the courage to apply. We evaluate past efforts and outcomes, and discard any that haven't seemed to work. We stay open to the idea that the child himself is learning and growing. Each child has no way of knowing that his experience is any different than others around him — and usually has only a limited way to let us know what those unique experiences, decisions, and beliefs are forming to build their world view.

Penny reminded me recently what truly makes these conversations special: the purity of intent. I love that: the purity of intent. There is no formulaic response to apply to each child at a given point in his or her development. There is all of our experience, our knowledge, our intuition, and our own lens and woundedness — and the kids point out to us over and over again that those things aren't enough. Not enough to puzzle out the best learning support. Not enough to provide the flexibility to meet the changing needs and possibilities of a growing being who is singularly him or herself. It also takes our presence with

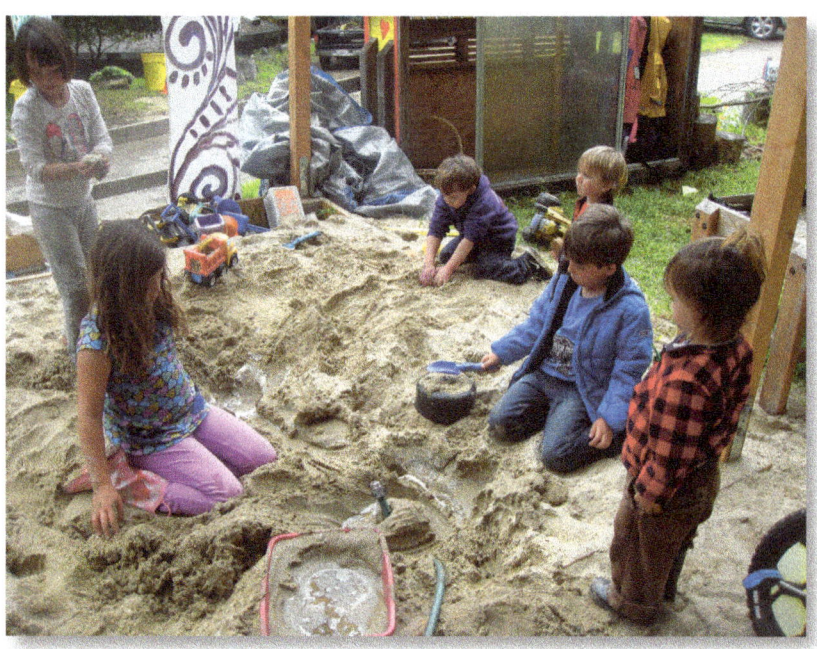

this moment — what does this situation call for? What is the child learning in this moment? How does this provide for their future? What about ourselves is getting in the way for these questions to be asked with the kids best interests always at the center? And our intent? On our good days, it is to provide the best learning environment possible to each of our little ones, and all that that includes. And so our conversations can run deep and wide, coming back to that purity, that focus, that guiding light. Are we providing that for this child, today? And each other?

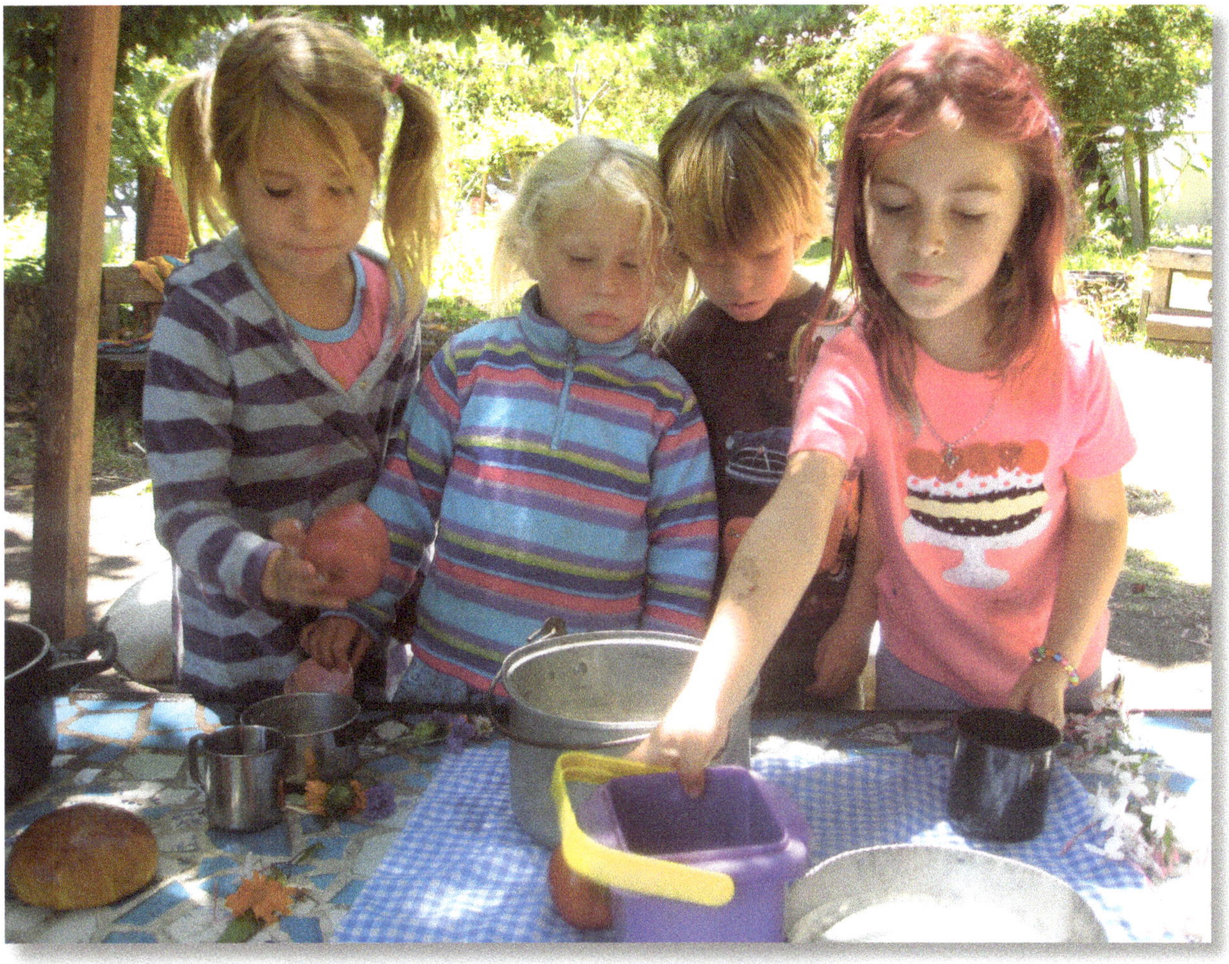

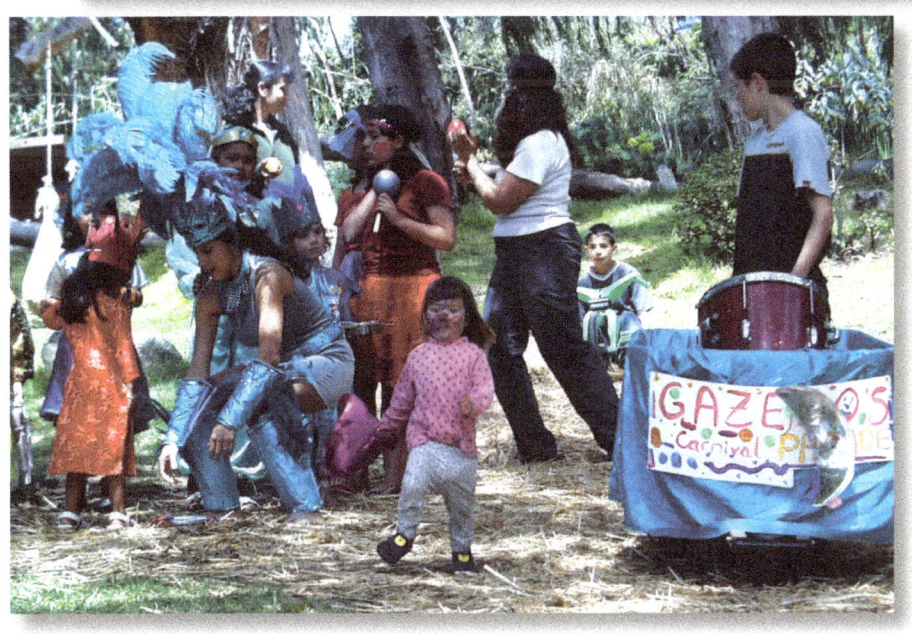

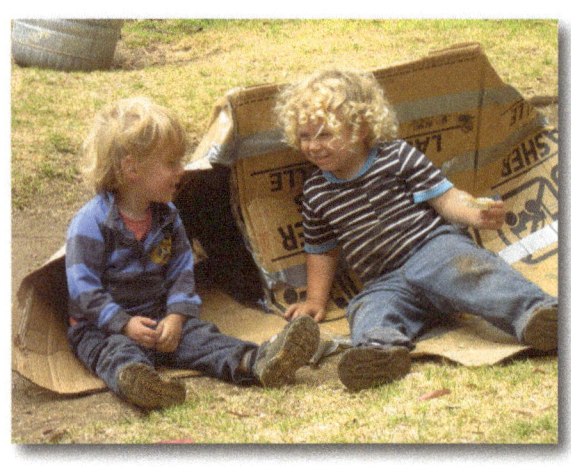

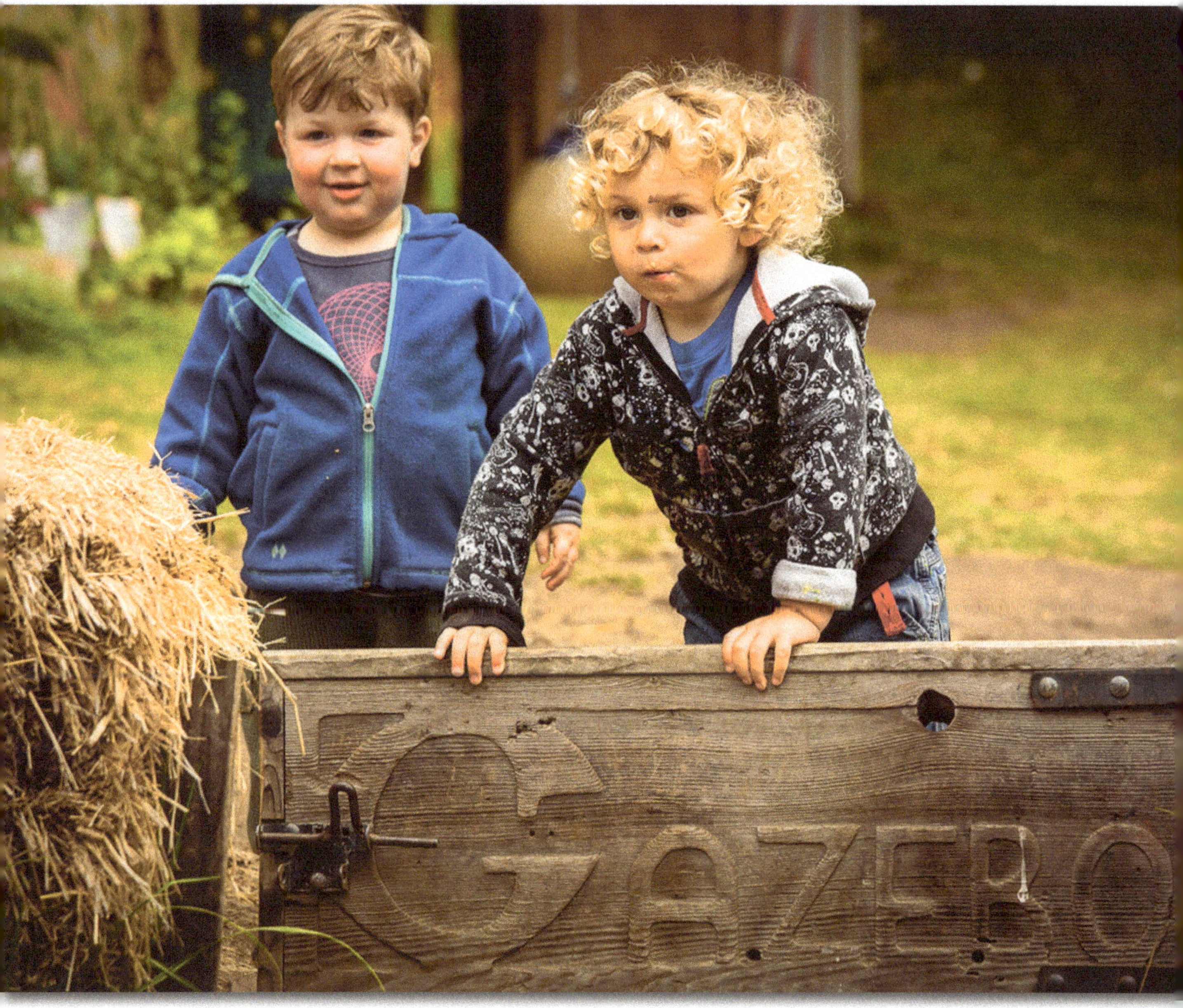

TODDLER LOVE

I have been delighted to watch two of our regular toddlers and their loving and not-so-loving interactions. They scream in delight when they first start their day, bumping into an embrace that embodies the word "toddle." They grab for the same toys, crying and shouting, to lose interest as something else grabs their eyes and attention, even as I feel the inclination to intervene. They tumble like puppies, covered in water and sand, giggling, then crying, then using their brilliance and a limited vocabulary to communicate intricate ideas of planning, sharing and feelings. They stand stock still, riveted by thoughts, sounds, movements of beast or butterfly, when seconds before their entire beings were one constant motion. They yell "NO!" even when they mean "yes." They say "mine" for every thing that could possibly be recognized. They stubbornly ignore their bodies' signals until their bodies' needs overcome them. Then they look for each other at snack to begin the cycles of giggles and shouts all over again. They teach us each day with their open affection, shared upsets, and glory in the present moment.

I love their toddler love.

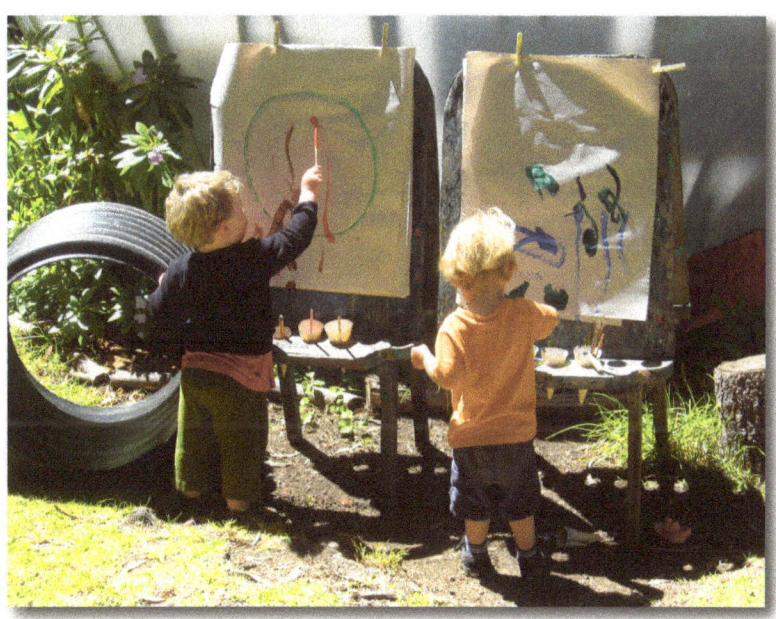

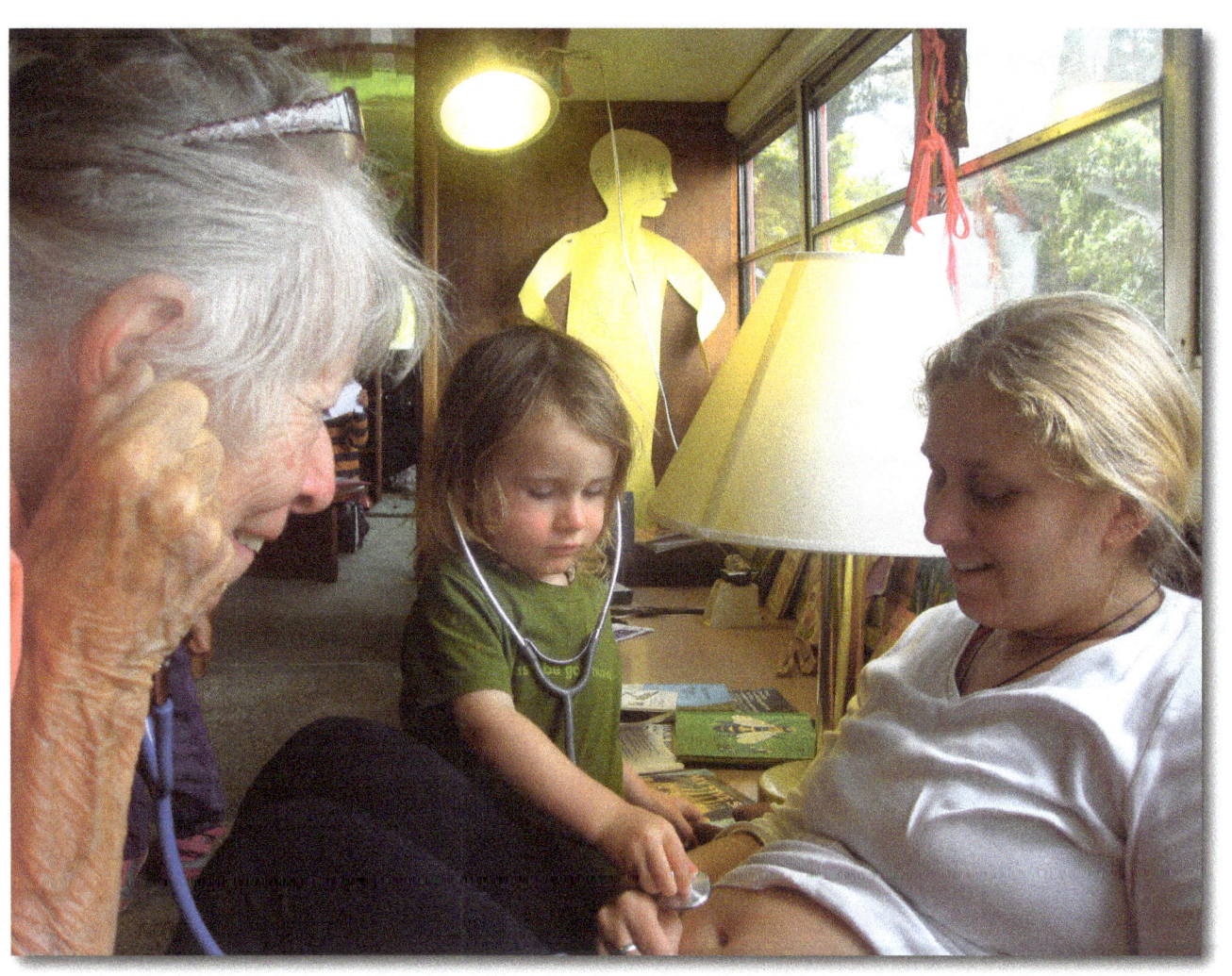

TEACH WHAT THE CHILDREN ARE INTERESTED IN

by Penny Vieregge

A 3 year old in the Focus Bus announces that her dentist found 9 cavities. My first thought is, "We are teaching incorrectly. What is missing?" The answer is immediate: "MINDFULNESS."

So we start being acquainted with our teeth — the front biters and the grabbers with their sharp edges, the back grinders with their flat surfaces. We discuss how food pieces get stuck in our teeth. They rot and make stinky holes in our teeth. We look at and feel the spaces between our teeth where the food gets caught. They go up and down. The brush has to go up and down to get them out. What a surprise!

Right after we eat we use our tongues to feel the pieces of food and the fuzzies on our teeth. As we get the toothbrushes we chant the "action song." Then we use our wrist action to go up and down. When we finish, we use our tongues again to feel our REALLY CLEAN TEETH.

Love, Penny

P.S. A note from January: Penny, in her 85th year, has piloted this program with Gazebo, Big Sur Health Clinic, and with children at Captain Cooper Elementary School. I am ever in awe of her energy and passion for teaching and learning.

RITES OF PASSAGE AT GAZEBO

One delightful aspect of working with young children is that one is given opportunity at every moment to see the world with the fresh eyes and innocent regard of the learning being.

As children in Gazebo Park approach the challenges of mastering their bodies, their emotions, and their expressions, there are myriad ways for them to choose "self-assessment."

On their own, without any adult telling them it's time to test their knowledge or skills, they seek those activities that offer them a sense of how far they have come in their development.

I was given a beautiful illustration of this in the Art Gazebo one day. There is a spiral staircase from the lower level to a cozy loft. Some wise teacher in the past removed the bottom step so that there is a certain level of height and coordination needed to climb up those stairs.

I have seen many of the children as toddlers try to follow the older preschoolers up that ladder and practice climbing for some extended periods of time. I have marveled at the seemingly innate ability to choose tasks and activities that are the perfect challenge to the child's own development range. These span the areas of emotional, social, physical, creative and cognitive domains of growth.

On this day, two children were engaged in a series of different types of play. I was sweeping the floor as the older child easily climbed up the stairs, only stopping as the younger child called out, "I can't do it, help me." The older child looked down on the younger with a slight disbelief on her face: "Just climb up. Just jump!" The younger child tried several times, saying, "I can't!" After watching for several more moments, I suggested to the older that she could teach or show the younger what she knows about climbing the stairs. She came back down and actually sort of stuttered in her own abilities as she was trying to both do the climb with thought, and explain verbally what she was doing. She even tried pushing him up from behind. This process took over 15 minutes. Eventually they both went on to some other mutual activity and I was left marveling at how a mixed-age classroom gives opportunity for the "teacher" to solidify their own learning by having to explain it. The human being is equipped with a beautiful inborn drive to become his or her full potential. Once again, Gazebo has renewed my faith in the self-driven curriculum, and the self-awarded satisfaction in mastery.

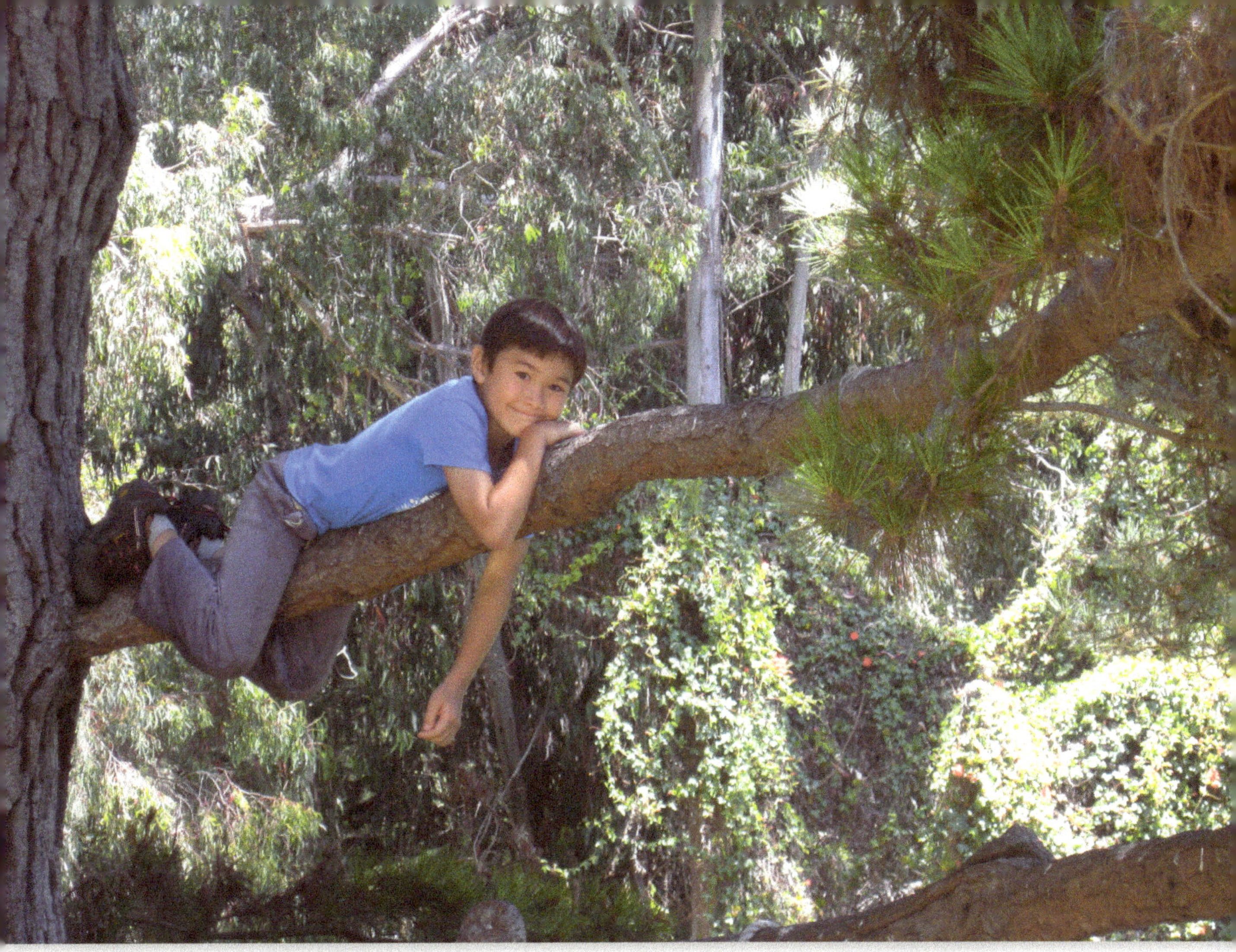

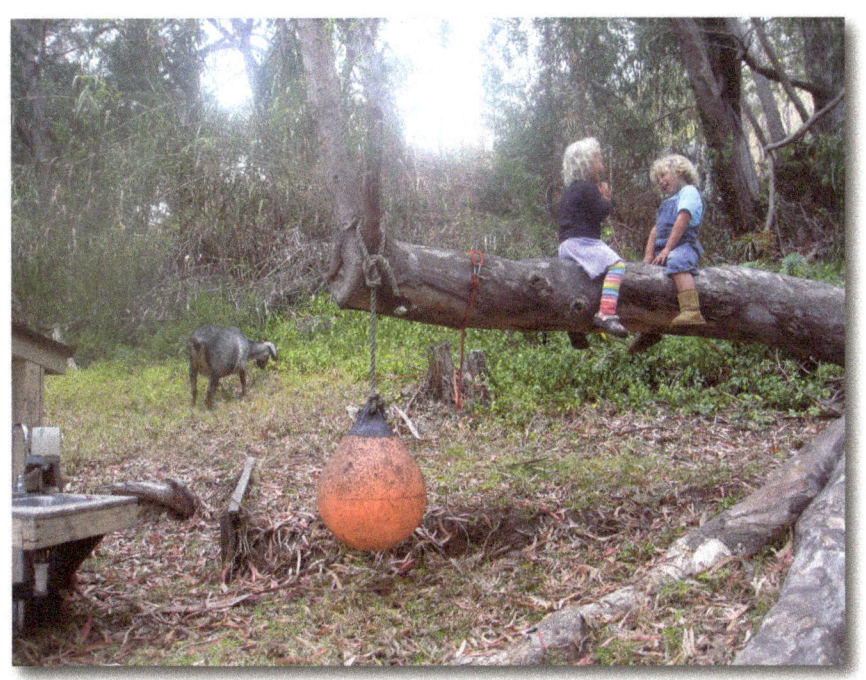

TODDLER DETECTIVE

I have been captivated by a new 18-month old student at Gazebo: "Ms. A." I find myself enthralled by her intense and wide-ranging exploration and how much it reminds me of what we so quickly grow to take for granted. It also is a clear example of how much of our drive toward discovery and development comes from within.

I watched Ms. A work for several minutes to get the block cupboard open, fiddling and re-fiddling with the latch. When it opened she let out a delighted, "Aw!" and then focused her attention on getting out a box of blocks. Even for the teachers these boxes must be wiggled just so to find space on the shelves. After a prolonged period with appropriate grunts and growls, she let out a wail. I immediately (my mistake was the immediately part) offered, "I am here if you want help." She responded with a firm shake of her head, "No!" She then spent the next minutes with more furious determination, and finally got the box out, "DAW!" she exclaimed with a triumphant look on her face. She then dumped all the blocks out, and put them back one by one, and repeated this circle several times, before one final emptying process.

Later Ms. A toddled up to the art gazebo, and after a painstaking climb up into the art space she dry painted on every imaginable surface with brushes she took in and out of the brush container, with seemingly no expectation of wet or color impact. Ms. A then went up and down the rainbow bridge stairs, in that step and catch up, step and catch up way toddlers do. She stomped her feet quite firmly, listening to the sounds her shoes made upon the wooden stairs. She then noticed the blue tumbling mat left out to dry from yesterday's slip-n-slide in which the older children had engaged. Now, having the dry mat all to herself, she marched up and down it, watching her feet, and then stepping off onto the grass, then back on, over and over, with a funneled focus. Suddenly some of the magnet tiles in the grass caught her attention, and standing next to another toddler who was both mouthing them, and trying to talk, Ms. A tried to fit them in the holes for paint containers of the easel. She emitted babbles in a seemingly wordless exchange with the nearby child.

A teacher was in the sound garden with another child, and Ms. A toddled over (falling at least 3 times) on the bumpy grass to grab for the mallet stick used on the xylophone and hanging bells and pans — only she used it striking the grass, pinging the strings by which the metal objects

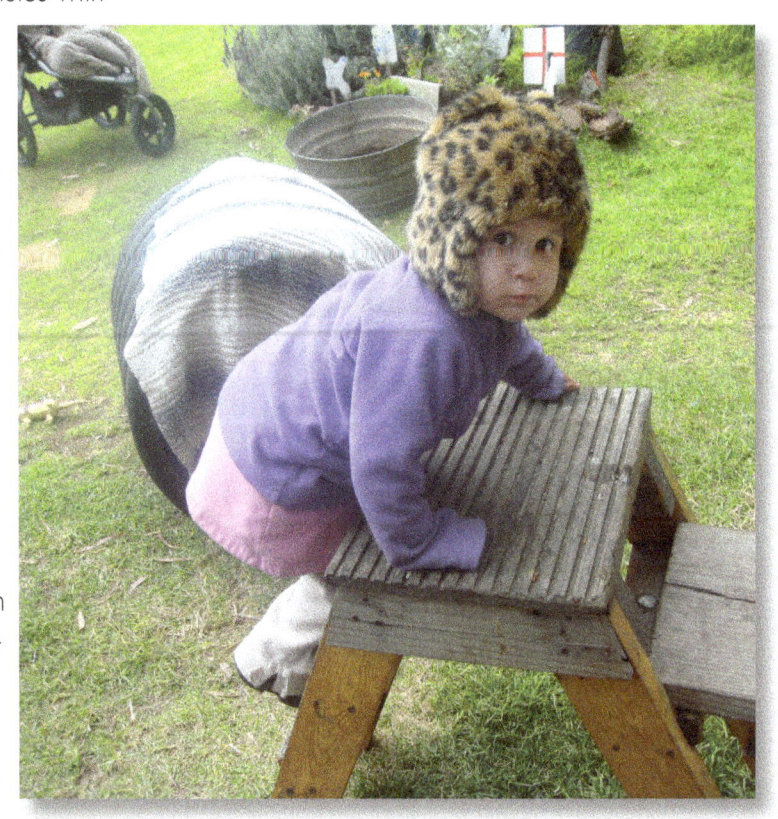

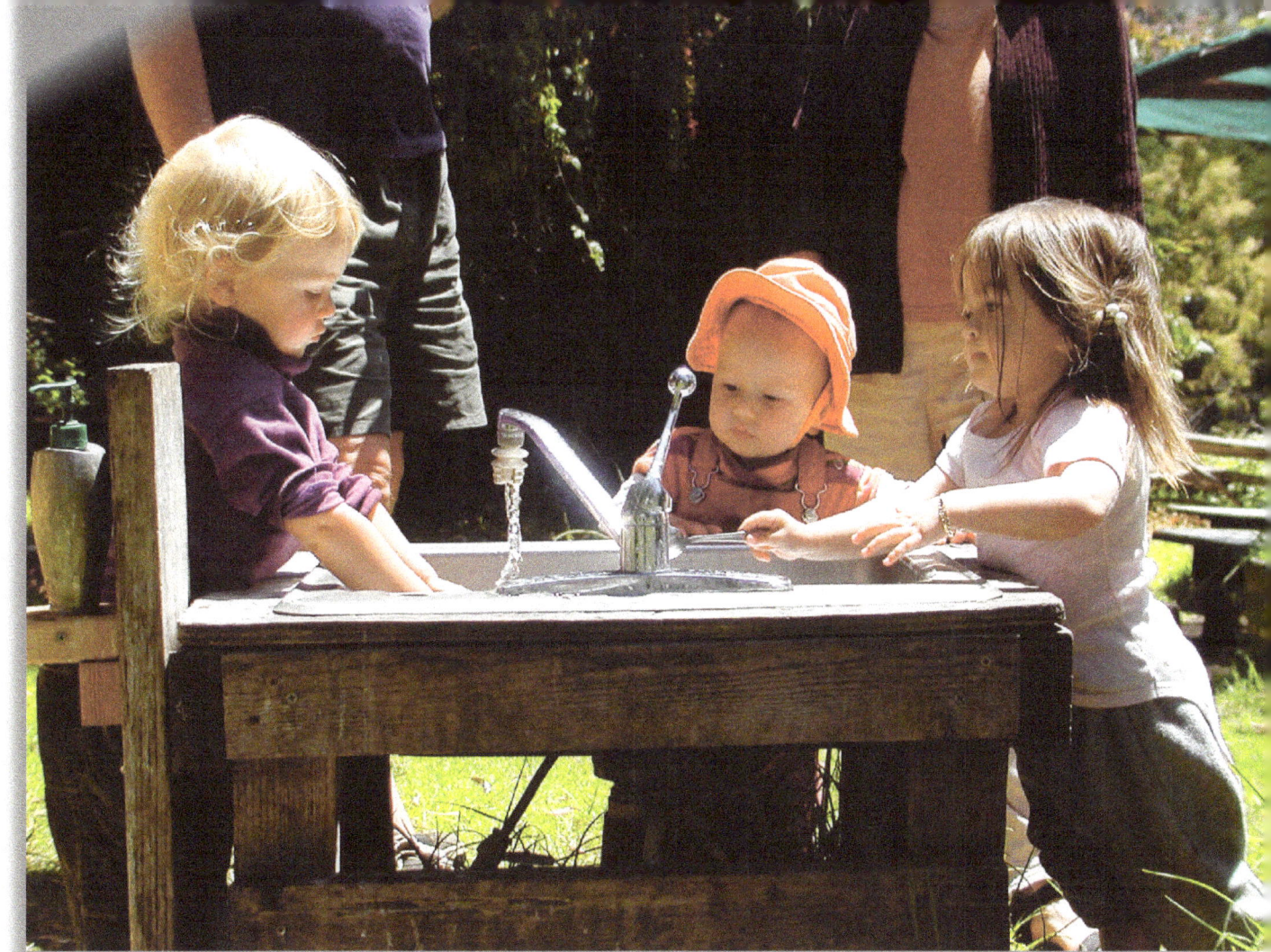

hung, pattering the fence, and knocking on the wooden sculpture. I realized that none of these things would have been explored if I had led the way with my own adult ideas of what was to be learned.

On another day, inside the farmhouse, Ms. A danced on the wooden floor, bouncing with feet seemingly glued to one place, hands flapping, a big beautiful grin gracing her face. She wanted her socks off, and to feel the floor. She walked watching her feet. She then went to the entrance and noticed all the lined-up shoes, trying on many of the teachers' slip-ons. She tromped around delighted with herself, checking out our responses by peering upward with a hopeful light at our smiles and laughter. She turned around to let herself down backwards over the big step, then went right back to pulling herself up, one knee coming up under her to propel her forward. I often get exhausted (and truthfully, sometimes bored) witnessing the repetition by which toddlers do the needed practice and gross motor/small motor motions needed to develop the muscles that they use to move their amazing bodies toward and away from interest and stimulation. Repetition and novelty, motion and rest, in relationship with others or the land, or in an island of focus and fascination — these determined detectives illuminate the beauty of our complex work with following the lead of a body that knows what is needed next to grow.

GOING ON ADVENTURES, GAZEBO-STYLE

About every 2 weeks or so, Gazebo Park School appears abandoned, as we pack up our gear and curiosity and go on an "adventure!" We stuff diapers, wipes, the radio, and first aide kit into a bag. We don sun hats and acquire treasures of flowers, rocks, or feathers we find along the way. Teachers and children set forth to explore the great land of Esalen on our way to lunch on the front lawn. Last week we saw seed pods of huge variety and marveled how nature makes seeds that hitchhike, parachute, helicopter, and find other ways of traveling from their place of origin. We tasted the nectar of the passionflowers as we saw hummingbirds do the same. We launched leafy fairy boats in the stream to watch them tumble down the cascades that cooled our bare feet. We trudged up hills that had trees draping moss messages over our heads. We lay on our stomachs at the pond to see which birds were visiting there, or which fish or larvae might show themselves. We picked celery in the garden we washed and munched as one of the children led us into the "secret" rose garden. We asked the farmers about their fascinating tools as they worked on what could be our lunch or dinner that day. We fed the chickens grass and heard the rooster crow, loudly enough to make us all startle and laugh. And this was just one way!

Throughout it all I watched teachers dance in and out of the children's discoveries, asking a focusing question, thinking out loud about comparisons, placing their bodies so children could discover their own balance and disequilibrium while still providing subtle safety boundaries. And slowing down, and slowing down, and slowing down some more. Because the curriculum unfolded as the bud does — from the inside out — the little ones show us what each is working on, curious toward or learning about, in their own ways of knowing. Because each piece of the adventure tends to be initiated by a child, and each transition to the next activity is also initiated by a child, the flow lends itself to deeper learning that is integrated to each child's unique understanding of the world. Because we can give this gift of timelessness, of this beautiful "now" moment, the child's bio-clock and development are honored. When that respect is offered to learning and growing, the magic of being human shows some of its greatest potential. On the way back we often return to the production clock and sing, sling, and nudge the children toward the "real life" time that waits in the world their families must negotiate each day. I have become more and more aware of how precious each of these adventures is; the most bountiful seeds are planted in the potential of the child's own unfolding. We teachers in the outdoor classroom are ever witnessing the process of natural growth in all the little buds we nurture.

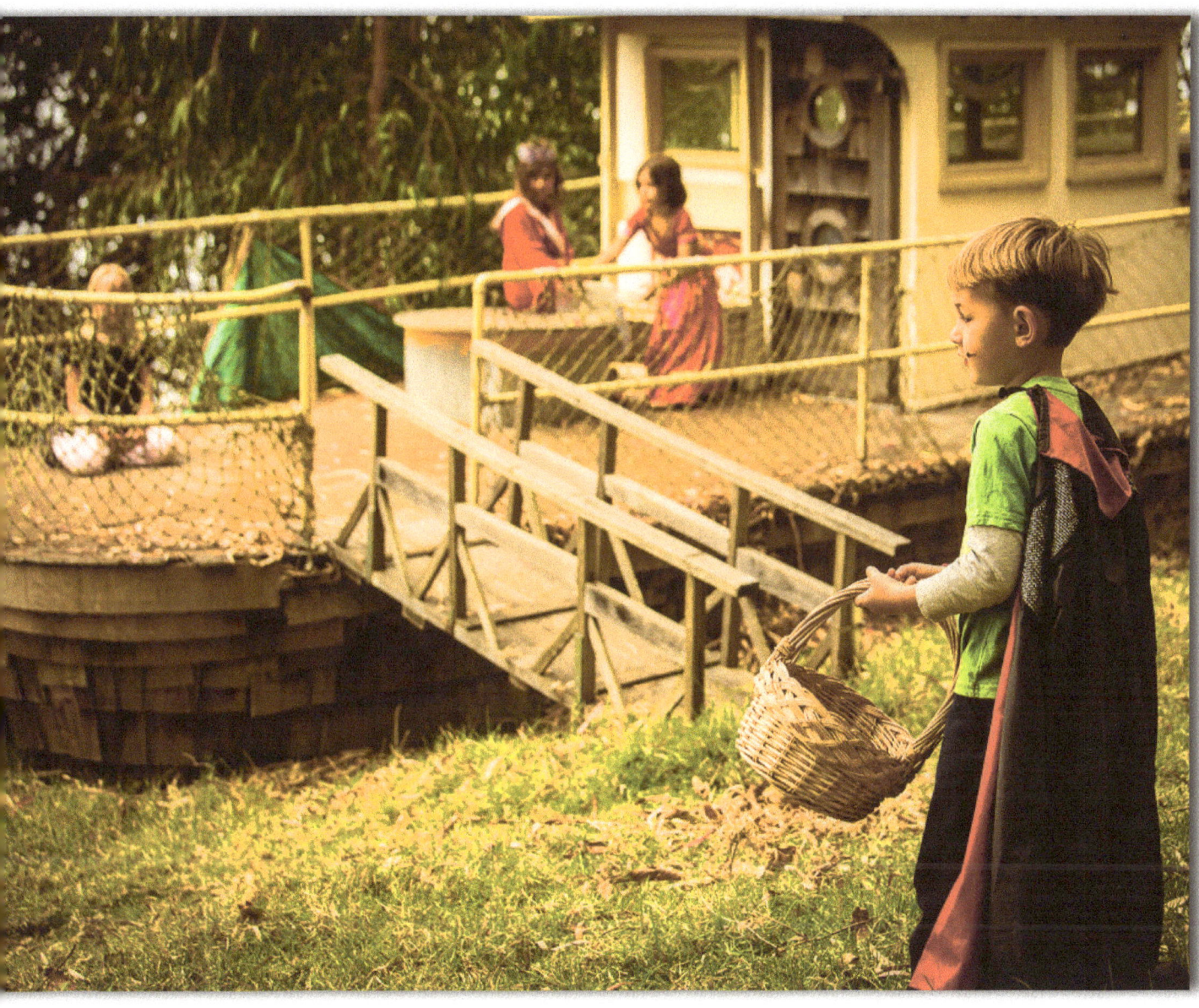

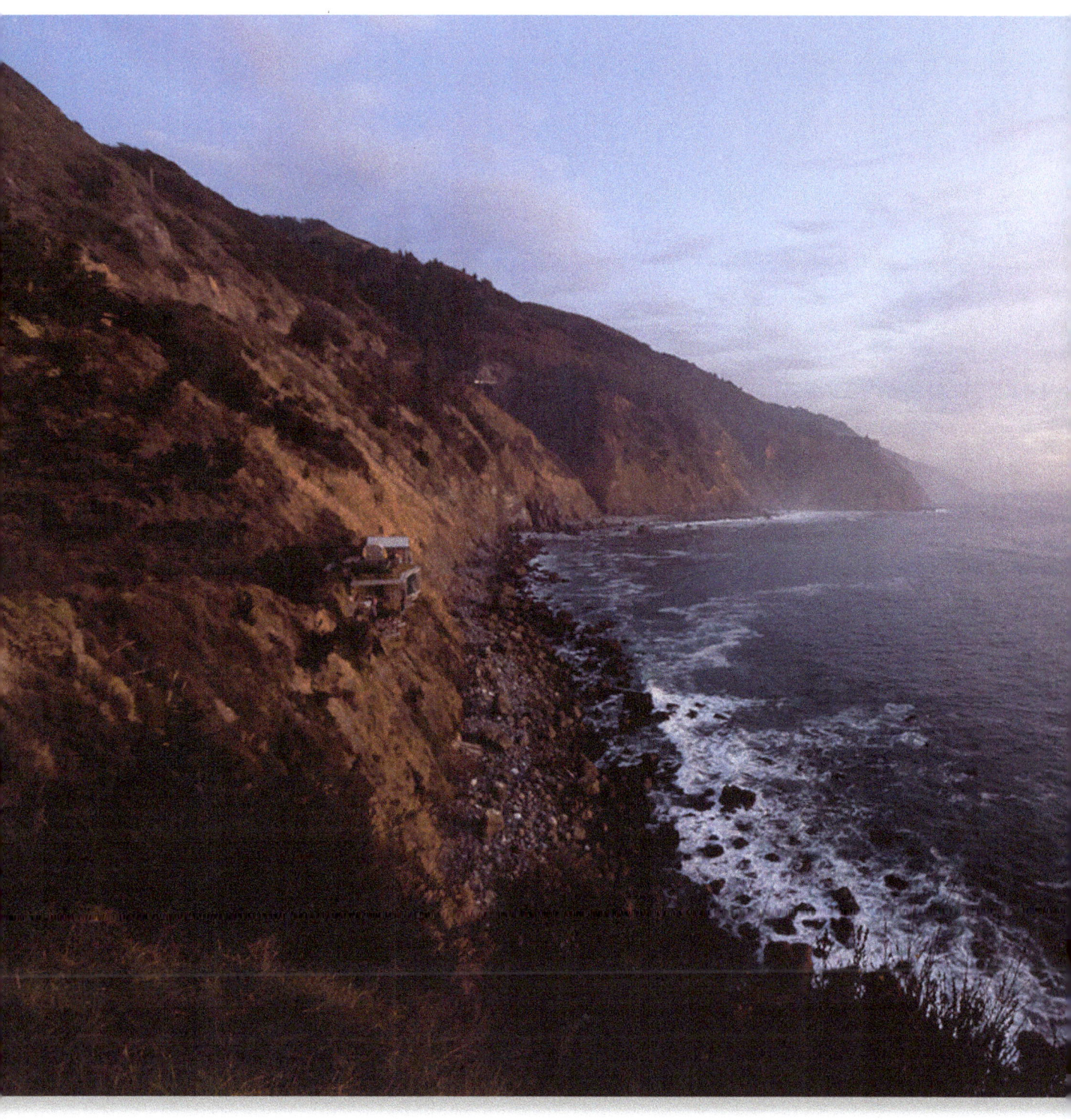

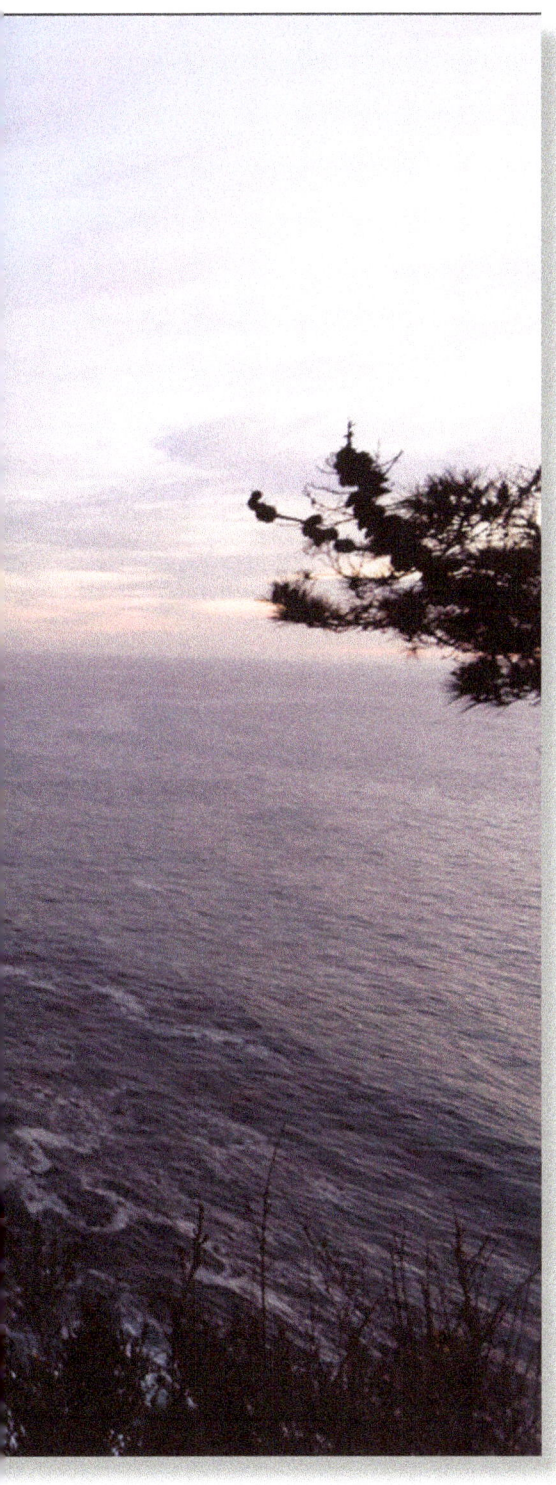

WATCHING THE SEASONS AT GAZEBO

I have to take just a moment to acknowledge that Gazebo is located in heaven. Truly, these mostly sunny winter days have hundreds of monarch butterflies dancing through the crisp air, with gray whales spouting and surfacing just off our rugged cliffs where the Pacific Ocean's breath keeps the air fresh. There is no place at Esalen where we can walk with the children that isn't an awe-inspiring view, with sunlit mountain tops, organic gardens and farmland, or magical deep redwood forests that line the creek carved canyons.

While I observe the children, I focus with them down to the tiny, beautiful flora and small creatures that populate the world often missed by the grown-up eyes that focus outward. They have taught me that whether I am lying on the lawn in a backyard of suburbia, looking out the window of a bus, or even riding a tricycle on an asphalt pathway, nature's beauty and intricate systems are abundant and informative, everywhere.

From macro to micro, following the children's interests leads us back over and over again to the greatest parts of being human — the parts that no standardized test can ever capture: creativity, curiosity, imagination, passion, relationship, wonder, love!

And I am deeply grateful I work at a place where we can feel the rhythms of the earth in such profound and beautiful ways.

WEATHER REPORTS FROM GAZEBO

At Gazebo the daily weather report is derived from an Esalen-wide ritual, which often has little to do with the actual constantly changing Big Sur climate. Each day, after families have been greeted and children have begun their day, the teachers gather in a circle to do a check-in. The check-in has a few deeper purposes besides the friendly "how-do-you-dos" they might seem to be to the casual observer. This is also done at the beginning of any staff meetings, or group process. I've come to treasure this ritual, and to see how it could truly benefit just about any work place. Except Gazebo is not any workplace. It is steeped in the need for consciousness, self-reflection, humility, and emotional presence, as every nuance of the park impacts the children who are in our charge.

In order for these little ones to develop to potential, we teachers must be willing to do the constant work of our own development. This mirrors the opportunities and challenges that every parent is offered throughout their children's growing years, and, as I'm finding out with my grown children, throughout their lives. The children listen to our words, hear our expressions of emotion, and even more importantly, read our every non-verbal cue as to what is going on within and among us. The space we hold for each other's unique package of strengths and struggles, the encouragement and support offered, and the way that problems and conflict are approached, provide the actual neural connections that will be the foundation for all future learning, for all future relationships.

We take this time each morning, modeling its importance by stating to children that we are doing teacher check-in so they can wait for help or solve questions themselves. This not only offers them the opportunity to work things out themselves with the added esteem and resourcefulness that supplies, but indicates that the teachers value each other, and the work we do with the children in the park. We stay conscious of little ears, and we share without interruption (well, mostly without interruption) how each of us is doing, and what support we need or can offer each other as teammates.

After we get a summary of each staff member's emotional temperature and their requests and offerings, we turn to the business of the day: Who is cooking lunch? Who wants to take early break? What land stewardship jobs need attention today? Any messages from parents that we all need to know? Then, as we move into the day of delight with the children, we also carry each other's well-being. Then the depth of growth of every member of our learning community deepens beyond any other setting where I have worked — even when the weather in Big Sur is stormy!

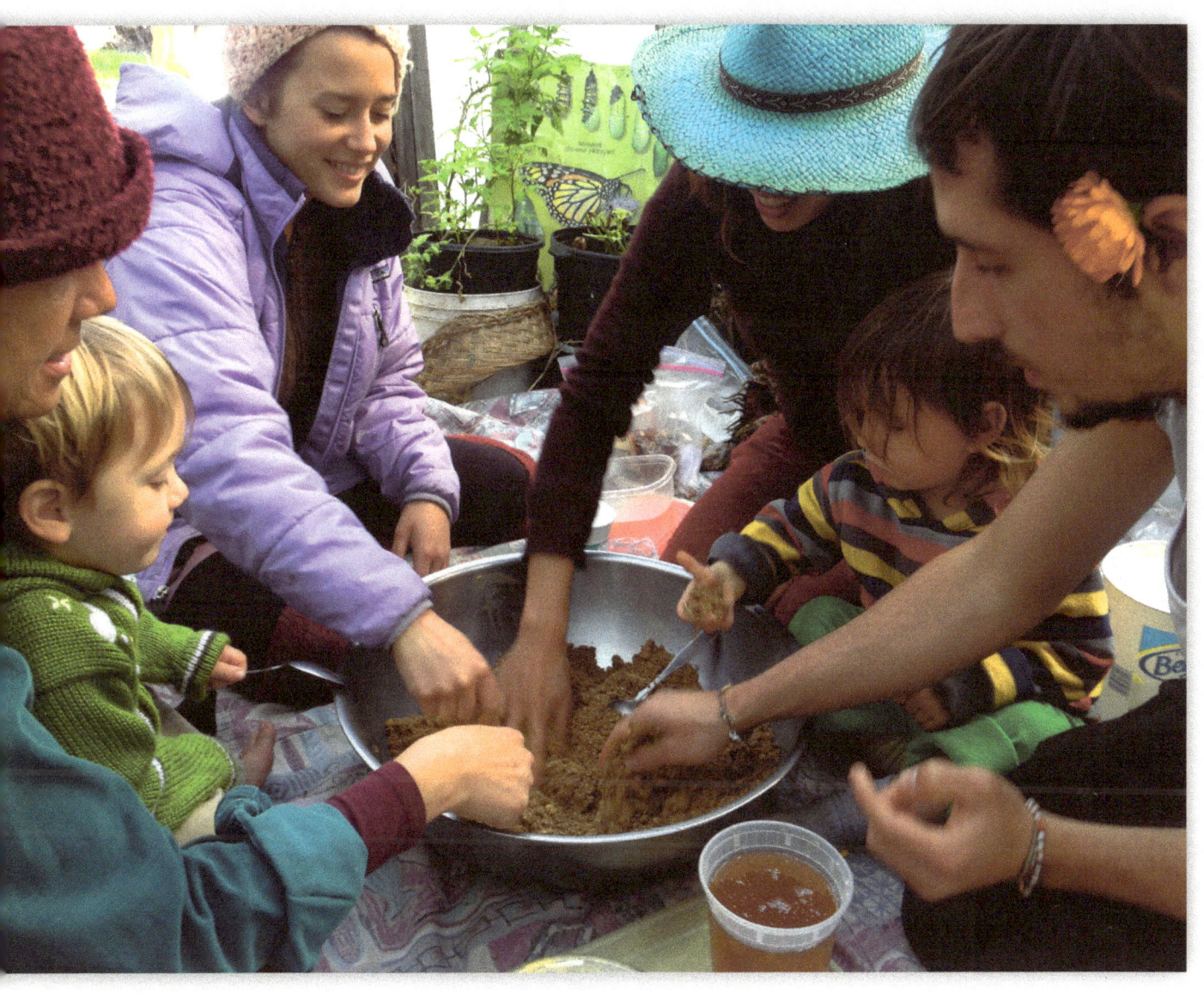

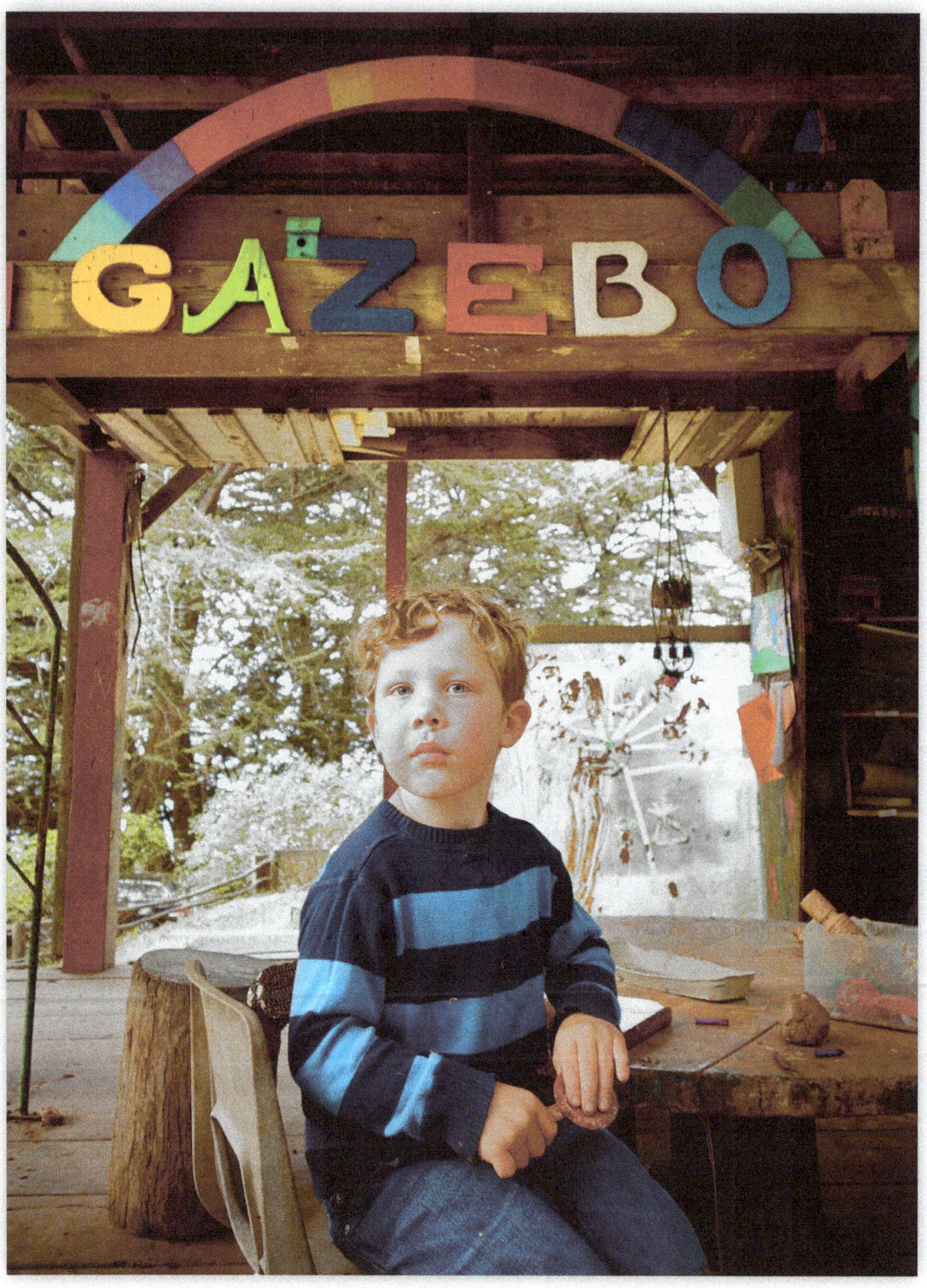

A YEAR OF GROWING WITH GAZEBO

At the end of May I will have had my first year at Gazebo, living and working at Esalen, and in the Big Sur Area. I am not the same person, nor educator who came here a year ago. It sounds so obvious but Gazebo grows grown-ups as much or more than it does the children who come here. So many factors come into play but I'd like to share my short list, after 31 years of being a parent, and 25+ years of being a teacher and parent educator, of the diamond-edged aspects that carve and sculpt the beings who are lucky enough to experience Gazebo.

1. The land and animals/land stewardship/eco-conscious curriculum:

Better artists than I have tried to express the power of this range of mountain and sea. Suffice it to say the land here is always teaching, always asking us to stretch beyond ourselves, always offering metaphor and magic.

2. The Gestalt overlay: As my understanding of Gestalt awareness practice and process has deepened, so has my respect for the support it offers in communication, self-self and self-other understanding, body wisdom and presence in the here and now.

3. Freedom, risk and trust: I have always loved we human beings and our complexity and potentials, always felt that we have deep knowing of our own needed pathway and areas of growing. Here the children offer me daily proof of how these unique characteristics of Gazebo nurture capable, confident beings who tackle problem-solving and conflict resolution with vulnerability, humor, relish, and resiliency.

4. Community-based learning: To be surrounded by Esalen and the greater Big Sur community that offers a necessary cooperation, sharing, and respect for the land has renewed my enthusiasm for learning in the circle — a continuous exchange of energy, ideas, feelings, dreams, and gratitude.

Here's to the coming year and all it holds for Gazebo, its staff and our beloved community.

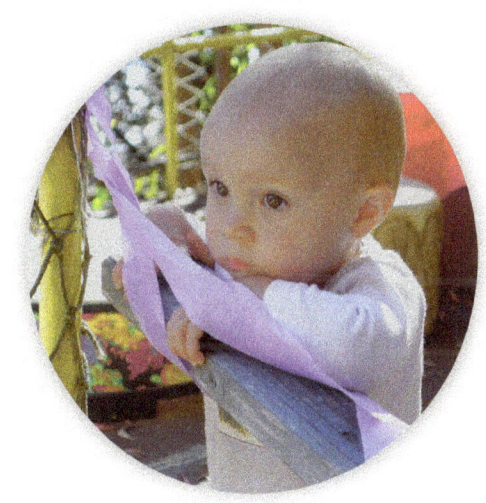

GAZEBO PARK SCHOOL

email: gazebo@esalen.org

www.esalen.org • (831) 667-3026

Contributing photographers:
Doug Ellis, David Gilmore
Book design: David Gilmore
Book production: River Sanctuary Publishing

www.ingramcontent.com/pod-product-compliance
Lightning Source LLC
Chambersburg PA
CBHW040548220526
45473CB00017B/3050